Collins Assessment

Spelling Half Termly Tests

Year 1/P2

Clare Dowdall

William Collins' dream of knowledge for all began with the publication of his first book in 1819.
A self-educated mill worker, he not only enriched millions of lives, but also founded a flourishing
publishing house. Today, staying true to this spirit, Collins books are packed with inspiration,
innovation and practical expertise. They place you at the centre of a world of possibility
and give you exactly what you need to explore it.

Collins. Freedom to teach.

Collins
An imprint of HarperCollins*Publishers*
The News Building
1 London Bridge Street
London
SE1 9GF

Browse the complete Collins catalogue at **www.collins.co.uk**

© HarperCollins*Publishers* Limited 2018

10 9 8 7 6 5 4 3 2 1

ISBN 978-0-00-831150-6

All rights reserved. No part of this publication may be reproduced, stored in a retrieval system,
or transmitted in any form by any means, electronic, mechanical, photocopying, recording or otherwise,
without the prior written permission of the Publisher or a licence permitting restricted copying in
the United Kingdom issued by the Copyright Licensing Agency Ltd., Barnard's Inn, 86 Fetter Lane, London, EC4A 1EN.

British Library Cataloguing in Publication Data. A catalogue record for this publication is available from the British Library.

Author: Clare Dowdall
Publisher: Katie Sergeant
Senior Editor: Mike Appleton
Copyeditor: Tanya Solomons
Proofreader: Catherine Dakin
Cover designer: The Big Mountain Design, Ken Vail Graphic Design
Production controller: Katharine Willard

Contents

How to use this book   4

Year 1/P2 Word Lists
Autumn Half Term 1   6
Autumn Half Term 2   8
Spring Half Term 1   10
Spring Half Term 2   12
Summer Half Term 1   14
Summer Half Term 2   16

Year 1/P2 Half Termly Tests
Autumn Half Term 1 Test A   18
Autumn Half Term 1 Test B   21
Autumn Half Term 2 Test A   24
Autumn Half Term 2 Test B   27
Spring Half Term 1 Test A   30
Spring Half Term 1 Test B   33
Spring Half Term 2 Test A   36
Spring Half Term 2 Test B   39
Summer Half Term 1 Test A   42
Summer Half Term 1 Test B   45
Summer Half Term 2 Test A   48
Summer Half Term 2 Test B   51

Answers
Answers in Context   54
Word-only Answers   66

Year 1/P2 Spelling Record Sheet   67

How to use this book

Introduction

Collins Assessment Spelling Half Termly Tests have been designed to give you a consistent whole school approach to teaching and assessing spelling. Each photocopiable book covers the required rules, words and common exception words from the English National Curriculum statutory guidance and Spelling Appendix. For teachers in Scotland, the books can offer guidance and structure that is not provided in the Curriculum for Excellence Experiences and Outcomes or Benchmarks.

Revision of previous years' work is also included, where appropriate, to ensure children are building their skills to become confident and secure spellers. As standalone tests, independent of any teaching and learning scheme, *Collins Assessment Spelling Half Termly Tests* provide a structured way to assess progress in spelling, to identify areas for development, and to provide evidence towards expectations for each year group.

Why spelling matters

Spelling is a key focus of the 2014 English National Curriculum statutory requirements for writing, and the expectations and demands are significant. Out of a possible 70 marks, 20 are awarded for spelling in the Key Stage 2 National Tests, and 20 per cent of the new English Language GCSE 9–1 marks are allocated to spelling, punctuation and grammar. In Year 2, there is an optional Key Stage 1 English grammar, punctuation and spelling test that schools can use to help them make an assessment about children's spelling knowledge, as well as looking at their writing. In Scotland, the P1 literacy, P4 writing and P7 writing Scottish National Standardised Assessments assess spelling at early, first and second levels, respectively.

Focusing on spelling knowledge and skills will also benefit children's wider writing and will have a lasting impact across their education in primary, secondary and beyond. The *Collins Assessment Spelling Half Termly Tests* aim to support teachers to make assessments about children's confidence and use of required spelling rules and strategies, in order to support preparation for these standard assessment points.

How to use this book

The book is divided into two main sections. In the first section, between 30 and 36 weekly word lists are provided (depending on the year group). Each list contains six to ten words per half term. These words can be used for weekly tests and used in the classroom, or sent home with the children. They generally follow the order of the spelling rules as set out in the Spelling Appendix of the National Curriculum and include any words that are specified in the word lists and the non-statutory guidance.

In the second section, 12 half-termly tests are provided, offering two test options per half term: Test A and Test B. These tests offer an equivalent level of challenge and are designed to cover the spelling patterns for that half term's work. The spellings in the half-termly tests are presented in a random order within contextualised sentences. The sentences used are appropriate for the year group in terms of content, grammar and punctuation. The tests are designed to build experience and confidence with this format as well as to test children's spelling knowledge when writing in context.

Each test should take approximately 10–15 minutes. Guidance is provided for each test, with instructions to read out to the children and a script. The children write the word in the gap in the sentence on their test.

How to use this book

The tests have been written to ensure smooth progression in children's spelling ability within the book and across the rest of the books in series, enabling them to build on their spelling knowledge and show progress.

Marking the tests

The answers are provided in two formats for ease of use: in context and in short form for quick marking.

Recording progress

You can use the pupil-facing record sheets to provide evidence of the areas in which children have performed well and where they need to focus. A spreadsheet is provided in the downloadable version so results can easily be recorded for your classes, and any gaps in understanding can be identified. The spreadsheet can then be used to inform your next teaching and learning steps.

Editable download

All the files are available in Word and PDF format for you to edit if you wish. Go to collins.co.uk/assessment/downloads to find instructions on how to download. The files are password protected and the password clue is included on the website. You will need to use the clue to locate the password in your book.

Year 1/P2 Word lists – Autumn Half Term 1

Word list 1

the
a
do
to
today
of

Word list 2

said
says
are
were
was
is

Word list 3

his
has
I
you
your
they

Year 1/P2 Word lists – Autumn Half Term 1

Word list 4

be
he
me
she
we
no
go
so

Word list 5

by
my
here
there
where
love
come
some

Word list 6

off
well
miss
buzz
back
if
pal
us
bus
yes

Year 1/P2 Word lists – Autumn Half Term 2

Word list 7

bank
tank
plank
think
sink
drink
honk
plonk
sunk
trunk

Word list 8

catch
hatch
fetch
kitchen
itch
ditch
pitch
notch
hutch
rich

Word list 9

which
much
such
have
live
give
save
cave
dive
five

Year 1/P2 Word lists – Autumn Half Term 2

Word list 10

cats
hats
dogs
spends
bricks
rocks
licks
thanks
catches
itches

Word list 11

hunting
hunted
hunter
buzzing
buzzed
buzzer
jumping
jumped
jumper
fizzing

Word list 12

grander
grandest
slower
slowest
fresher
freshest
quicker
quickest
softer
softest

Year 1/P2 Word lists – Spring Half Term 1

Word list 1

rain
wait
train
paid
afraid
oil
join
coin
point
soil

Word list 2

day
play
say
way
stay
away
boy
toy
enjoy
annoy

Word list 3

made
came
same
take
safe
these
theme
complete
toe
goes

Year 1/P2 Word lists – Spring Half Term 1

Word list 4
five
ride
like
time
side
home
those
woke
hope
hole

Word list 5
June
rule
rude
use
tube
tune
car
start
park
garden

Word list 6
see
tree
green
meet
week
sea
dream
meat
each
read

© HarperCollins*Publishers* Ltd 2018

Year 1/P2 Word lists – Spring Half Term 2

Word list 7	Word list 8	Word list 9
head	better	turn
bread	under	hurt
meant	summer	church
instead	winter	burst
read	sister	Thursday
tread	girl	food
her	bird	pool
term	shirt	moon
verb	first	zoo
person	third	soon

Year 1/P2 Word lists – Spring Half Term 2

Word list 10	Word list 11	Word list 12
book	out	own
took	about	blow
foot	mouth	snow
wood	around	grow
good	sound	show
boat	now	blue
coat	how	clue
road	brown	true
coach	down	rescue
goal	town	Tuesday

Year 1/P2 Word lists – Summer Half Term 1

Word list 1	Word list 2	Word list 3
new	lie	high
few	tie	night
grew	pie	light
flew	cried	bright
drew	tried	right
threw	dried	might
crew	chief	sight
pew	field	fright
stew	thief	tonight
blew	shield	tight

Year 1/P2 Word lists – Summer Half Term 1

Word list 4
for
short
born
horse
morning
more
score
before
wore
shore

Word list 5
saw
draw
yawn
crawl
paw
law
author
August
dinosaur
astronaut

Word list 6
air
fair
pair
hair
chair
dear
hear
beard
near
year

© HarperCollins*Publishers* Ltd 2018

Year 1/P2 Word lists – Summer Half Term 2

Word list 7	Word list 8	Word list 9
bear	very	when
pear	happy	where
wear	funny	which
bare	party	wheel
dare	family	while
care	smelly	sketch
share	dolphin	kit
scared	alphabet	skin
rare	phonics	frisky
glare	elephant	skim

Year 1/P2 Word lists – Summer Half Term 2

Word list 10	Word list 11	Word list 12
what	football	one
why	playground	once
our	farmyard	ask
unhappy	bedroom	friend
undo	blackberry	school
unload	handbag	put
unfair	snowman	push
unlock	seaside	pull
unkind	classroom	full
untrue	treetop	house

Year 1/P2 Autumn Half Term 1 Test A

Spelling rules and knowledge

- Common exception words
- The sound made by **ff**

Guidance for teachers

The test is designed to build experience and confidence with this format, as well as to test children's spelling knowledge.
The test should take approximately 10–15 minutes.
Children should have a copy of the test and a pencil to use.
Children with specific needs should be given appropriate support.
All children should be encouraged to have a go at spelling each word, using the strategies that they have learnt.
Remind the children to check their answers by asking: *Does it look right? Does it sound right?*
Avoid over-emphasising the spelling of each word as you read it.

> Read each word aloud, saying: *The word is…*
> Next, read the sentence that includes the word.
> Wait for the children to attempt to write the word.
> Re-read the word, saying: *The word is…*

Remind the children to check the word before moving to the next spelling.
At the end of the test, read each sentence again and encourage the children to check back.

Instructions for children

(You may like to read this to the children prior to the test.)

This is a spelling test to check your knowledge of the spelling patterns we have worked on this half term.
You need a pencil.
Please write your name, class and the date at the top of the test.
I will read a word out loud and then say it again in a sentence.
You should write the word in the gap in the sentence on your test.
I will read it again and give you time to check it.
Don't worry if you are not sure about a spelling. Have a go using the strategies we have learnt.
If you make a mistake, cross out the word and try again.

Words tested (5)

the, said, you, here, off

Year 1/P2 Autumn Half Term 1 Test A

Spelling script

Spelling 1: The word is **the**.
Eat **the** cake.
The word is **the**.

Spelling 2: The word is **said**.
The teacher **said**, "Hurry up!"
The word is **said**.

Spelling 3: The word is **you**.
Can **you** play the drums?
The word is **you**.

Spelling 4: The word is **here**.
Come **here** and sit down.
The word is **here**.

Spelling 5: The word is **off**.
The cat can jump **off** the bed.
The word is **off**.

Well done! Now I will read the sentences again so you can check your spelling.

| Name | Class | Date |

Year 1/P2 Autumn Half Term 1 Test A

1. Eat _____ cake.

2. The teacher _____, "Hurry up!"

3. Can _____ play the drums?

4. Come _____ and sit down.

5. The cat can jump _____ the bed.

Total _____ / 5

Year 1/P2 Autumn Half Term 1 Test B

Spelling rules and knowledge

- Common exception words
- The sound made by **zz**

Guidance for teachers

The test is designed to build experience and confidence with this format, as well as to test children's spelling knowledge.
The test should take approximately 10–15 minutes.
Children should have a copy of the test and a pencil to use.
Children with specific needs should be given appropriate support.
All children should be encouraged to have a go at spelling each word, using the strategies that they have learnt.
Remind the children to check their answers by asking: *Does it look right? Does it sound right?*
Avoid over-emphasising the spelling of each word as you read it.

> Read each word aloud, saying: *The word is…*
> Next, read the sentence that includes the word.
> Wait for the children to attempt to write the word.
> Re-read the word, saying: *The word is…*

Remind the children to check the word before moving to the next spelling.
At the end of the test, read each sentence again and encourage the children to check back.

Instructions for children

(You may like to read this to the children prior to the test.)

This is a spelling test to check your knowledge of the spelling patterns we have worked on this half term.
You need a pencil.
Please write your name, class and the date at the top of the test.
I will read a word out loud and then say it again in a sentence.
You should write the word in the gap in the sentence on your test.
I will read it again and give you time to check it.
Don't worry if you are not sure about a spelling. Have a go using the strategies we have learnt.
If you make a mistake, cross out the word and try again.

Words tested (5)

do, was, they, love, buzz

Year 1/P2 Autumn Half Term 1 Test B

Spelling script

Spelling 1: The word is **do**.
Do you like chocolate?
The word is **do**.

Spelling 2: The word is **was**.
He **was** feeling scared.
The word is **was**.

Spelling 3: The word is **they**.
They are best friends.
The word is **they**.

Spelling 4: The word is **love**.
We **love** our kitten.
The word is **love**.

Spelling 5: The word is **buzz**.
The wasp gave an angry **buzz**.
The word is **buzz**.

Well done! Now I will read the sentences again so you can check your spelling.

| Name | Class | Date |

Year 1/P2 Autumn Half Term 1 Test B

1. _____ you like chocolate?

2. He _____ feeling scared.

3. _____ are best friends.

4. We _____ our kitten.

5. The wasp gave an angry _____.

Total _____ / 5

Year 1/P2 Autumn Half Term 2 Test A

Spelling rules and knowledge

- The sound made by **n** before **k**
- The sound made by **tch** or sometimes **ch**
- The sound made by **v** at the end of words
- Adding **s** or **es** to make a word plural
- Adding **-ing**, **-ed**, **-er** to verbs where no change is needed to the root word
- Adding **-er** and **-est** to adjectives where no change is needed to the root word

Guidance for teachers

The test is designed to build experience and confidence with this format, as well as to test children's spelling knowledge.
The test should take approximately 10–15 minutes.
Children should have a copy of the test and a pencil to use.
Children with specific needs should be given appropriate support.
All children should be encouraged to have a go at spelling each word, using the strategies that they have learnt.
Remind the children to check their answers by asking: *Does it look right? Does it sound right?*
Avoid over-emphasising the spelling of each word as you read it.

> Read each word aloud, saying: *The word is...*
> Next, read the sentence that includes the word.
> Wait for the children to attempt to write the word.
> Re-read the word, saying: *The word is...*

Remind the children to check the word before moving to the next spelling.
At the end of the test, read each sentence again and encourage the children to check back.

Instructions for children

(You may like to read this to the children prior to the test.)

This is a spelling test to check your knowledge of the spelling patterns we have worked on this half term.
You need a pencil.
Please write your name, class and the date at the top of the test.
I will read a word out loud and then say it again in a sentence.
You should write the word in the gap in the sentence on your test.
I will read it again and give you time to check it.
Don't worry if you are not sure about a spelling. Have a go using the strategies we have learnt.
If you make a mistake, cross out the word and try again.

Words tested (6)

bank, catch, have, spends, hunted, slowest

Year 1/P2 Autumn Half Term 2 Test A

Spelling script

Spelling 1: The word is **bank**.
Be careful! The river **bank** may be slippery.
The word is **bank**.

Spelling 2: The word is **catch**.
Can we **catch** the fish?
The word is **catch**.

Spelling 3: The word is **have**.
Have you eaten your vegetables?
The word is **have**.

Spelling 4: The word is **spends**.
She **spends** her time playing on the computer.
The word is **spends**.

Spelling 5: The word is **hunted**.
The tiger **hunted** for its prey.
The word is **hunted**.

Spelling 6: The word is **slowest**.
The **slowest** runner came last in the race.
The word is **slowest**.

Well done! Now I will read the sentences again so you can check your spelling.

| Name | Class | Date |

Year 1/P2 Autumn Half Term 2 Test A

1. Be careful! The river _____ may be slippery.

2. Can we _____ the fish?

3. _____ you eaten your vegetables?

4. She _____ her time playing on the computer.

5. The tiger _____ for its prey.

6. The _____ runner came last in the race.

Total _____ / 6

Year 1/P2 Autumn Half Term 2 Test B

Spelling rules and knowledge

- The sound made by **n** before **k**
- The sound made by **tch** or sometimes **ch**
- The sound made by **v** at the end of words
- Adding **s** or **es** to make a word plural
- Adding **-ing**, **-ed**, **-er** to verbs where no change is needed to the root word
- Adding **-er** and **-est** to adjectives where no change is needed to the root word

Guidance for teachers

The test is designed to build experience and confidence with this format, as well as to test children's spelling knowledge.
The test should take approximately 10–15 minutes.
Children should have a copy of the test and a pencil to use.
Children with specific needs should be given appropriate support.
All children should be encouraged to have a go at spelling each word, using the strategies that they have learnt.
Remind the children to check their answers by asking: *Does it look right? Does it sound right?*
Avoid over-emphasising the spelling of each word as you read it.

> Read each word aloud, saying: *The word is…*
> Next, read the sentence that includes the word.
> Wait for the children to attempt to write the word.
> Re-read the word, saying: *The word is…*

Remind the children to check the word before moving to the next spelling.
At the end of the test, read each sentence again and encourage the children to check back.

Instructions for children

(You may like to read this to the children prior to the test.)

This is a spelling test to check your knowledge of the spelling patterns we have worked on this half term.
You need a pencil.
Please write your name, class and the date at the top of the test.
I will read a word out loud and then say it again in a sentence.
You should write the word in the gap in the sentence on your test.
I will read it again and give you time to check it.
Don't worry if you are not sure about a spelling. Have a go using the strategies we have learnt.
If you make a mistake, cross out the word and try again.

Words tested (6)

trunk, fetch, five, rocks, jumping, softer

Year 1/P2 Autumn Half Term 2 Test B

Spelling script

Spelling 1: The word is **trunk**.
The elephant's **trunk** snatched the doughnut.
The word is **trunk**.

Spelling 2: The word is **fetch**.
The dog loved to **fetch** its ball.
The word is **fetch**.

Spelling 3: The word is **five**.
One, two, three, four, **five**!
The word is **five**.

Spelling 4: The word is **rocks**.
The **rocks** at the beach were hard to climb.
The word is **rocks**.

Spelling 5: The word is **jumping**.
The kangaroo was **jumping** along the road.
The word is **jumping**.

Spelling 6: The word is **softer**.
My kitten's fur is **softer** than my teddy bear.
The word is **softer**.

Well done! Now I will read the sentences again so you can check your spelling.

| Name | Class | Date |

Year 1/P2 Autumn Half Term 2 Test B

1. The elephant's _____ snatched the doughnut.

2. The dog loved to _____ its ball.

3. One, two, three, four, _____!

4. The _____ at the beach were hard to climb.

5. The kangaroo was _____ along the road.

6. My kitten's fur is _____ than my teddy bear.

Total _____ / 6

Year 1/P2 Spring Half Term 1 Test A

Spelling rules and knowledge

- Vowel digraphs and trigraphs: **ai**, **oi**, **ay**, **oy**, **a-e**, **e-e**, **i-e**, **o-e**, **u-e**, **ee**

Guidance for teachers

The test is designed to build experience and confidence with this format, as well as to test children's spelling knowledge.
The test should take approximately 10–15 minutes.
Children should have a copy of the test and a pencil to use.
Children with specific needs should be given appropriate support.
All children should be encouraged to have a go at spelling each word, using the strategies that they have learnt.
Remind the children to check their answers by asking: *Does it look right? Does it sound right?*
Avoid over-emphasising the spelling of each word as you read it.

> Read each word aloud, saying: *The word is…*
> Next, read the sentence that includes the word.
> Wait for the children to attempt to write the word.
> Re-read the word, saying: *The word is…*

Remind the children to check the word before moving to the next spelling.
At the end of the test, read each sentence again and encourage the children to check back.

Instructions for children

(You may like to read this to the children prior to the test.)

This is a spelling test to check your knowledge of the spelling patterns we have worked on this half term.
You need a pencil.
Please write your name, class and the date at the top of the test.
I will read a word out loud and then say it again in a sentence.
You should write the word in the gap in the sentence on your test.
I will read it again and give you time to check it.
Don't worry if you are not sure about a spelling. Have a go using the strategies we have learnt.
If you make a mistake, cross out the word and try again.

Words tested (10)

rain, coin, play, boy, came, these, ride, woke, rule, tree

Year 1/P2 Spring Half Term 1 Test A

Spelling script

Spelling 1: The word is **rain**.
The **rain** washed the mud off the wellies.
The word is **rain**.

Spelling 2: The word is **coin**.
The shiny **coin** gleamed in my purse.
The word is **coin**.

Spelling 3: The word is **play**.
Let's **play** hide and seek.
The word is **play**.

Spelling 4: The word is **boy**.
The **boy** loved his new trainers.
The word is **boy**.

Spelling 5: The word is **came**.
The cheeky robin **came** close to my window.
The word is **came**.

Spelling 6: The word is **these**.
Whose smelly socks are **these**?
The word is **these**.

Spelling 7: The word is **ride**.
The camel **ride** was very bumpy!
The word is **ride**.

Spelling 8: The word is **woke**.
She **woke** up with a jump when the doorbell rang.
The word is **woke**.

Spelling 9: The word is **rule**.
The king liked to **rule** over his kingdom.
The word is **rule**.

Spelling 10: The word is **tree**.
The squirrels climbed up their favourite **tree** every morning.
The word is **tree**.

Well done! Now I will read the sentences again so you can check your spelling.

| Name | Class | Date |

Year 1/P2 Spring Half Term 1 Test A

1. The _____ washed the mud off the wellies.

2. The shiny _____ gleamed in my purse.

3. Let's _____ hide and seek.

4. The _____ loved his new trainers.

5. The cheeky robin _____ close to my window.

6. Whose smelly socks are _____?

7. The camel _____ was very bumpy!

8. She _____ up with a jump when the doorbell rang.

9. The king liked to _____ over his kingdom.

10. The squirrels climbed up their favourite _____ every morning.

Total _____ / 10

Year 1/P2 Spring Half Term 1 Test B

Spelling rules and knowledge

- Vowel digraphs and trigraphs: **ai**, **oi**, **ay**, **oy**, **a-e**, **oe**, **i-e**, **o-e**, **ar**, **ea**

Guidance for teachers

The test is designed to build experience and confidence with this format, as well as to test children's spelling knowledge.
The test should take approximately 10–15 minutes.
Children should have a copy of the test and a pencil to use.
Children with specific needs should be given appropriate support.
All children should be encouraged to have a go at spelling each word, using the strategies that they have learnt.
Remind the children to check their answers by asking: *Does it look right? Does it sound right?*
Avoid over-emphasising the spelling of each word as you read it.

> Read each word aloud, saying: *The word is…*
> Next, read the sentence that includes the word.
> Wait for the children to attempt to write the word.
> Re-read the word, saying: *The word is…*

Remind the children to check the word before moving to the next spelling.
At the end of the test, read each sentence again and encourage the children to check back.

Instructions for children

(You may like to read this to the children prior to the test.)

This is a spelling test to check your knowledge of the spelling patterns we have worked on this half term.
You need a pencil.
Please write your name, class and the date at the top of the test.
I will read a word out loud and then say it again in a sentence.
You should write the word in the gap in the sentence on your test.
I will read it again and give you time to check it.
Don't worry if you are not sure about a spelling. Have a go using the strategies we have learnt.
If you make a mistake, cross out the word and try again.

Words tested (10)

train, soil, away, enjoy, same, toe, side, hope, start, dream

Year 1/P2 Spring Half Term 1 Test B

Spelling script

Spelling 1: The word is **train**.
The **train** chugged into the tunnel.
The word is **train**.

Spelling 2: The word is **soil**.
We dug in the **soil** to plant our seeds.
The word is **soil**.

Spelling 3: The word is **away**.
The boys ran **away** from the barking dog.
The word is **away**.

Spelling 4: The word is **enjoy**.
I **enjoy** a cream cake with a cup of tea.
The word is **enjoy**.

Spelling 5: The word is **same**.
My new shoes are the **same** as yours.
The word is **same**.

Spelling 6: The word is **toe**.
Ouch! I stubbed my **toe** on the doorstep.
The word is **toe**.

Spelling 7: The word is **side**.
Put your shoes on at the **side** of the football pitch.
The word is **side**.

Spelling 8: The word is **hope**.
We **hope** that we can play outside today.
The word is **hope**.

Spelling 9: The word is **start**.
Toot your horn when you **start** the car.
The word is **start**.

Spelling 10: The word is **dream**.
I like to **dream** that I am on a beautiful beach.
The word is **dream**.

Well done! Now I will read the sentences again so you can check your spelling.

| Name | Class | Date |

Year 1/P2 Spring Half Term 1 Test B

1. The _____ chugged into the tunnel.

2. We dug in the _____ to plant our seeds.

3. The boys ran _____ from the barking dog.

4. I _____ a cream cake with a cup of tea.

5. My new shoes are the _____ as yours.

6. Ouch! I stubbed my _____ on the doorstep.

7. Put your shoes on at the _____ of the football pitch.

8. We _____ that we can play outside today.

9. Toot your horn when you _____ the car.

10. I like to _____ that I am on a beautiful beach.

Total _____ / 10

Year 1/P2 Spring Half Term 2 Test A

Spelling rules and knowledge

- Vowel digraphs and trigraphs: **ea** (*bread*), **er**, **er** (unstressed schwa), **ir**, **ur**, **oo** (*moon*), **oo** (*book*), **oa**, **ou**, **ow** (*grow*)

Guidance for teachers

The test is designed to build experience and confidence with this format, as well as to test children's spelling knowledge.
The test should take approximately 10–15 minutes.
Children should have a copy of the test and a pencil to use.
Children with specific needs should be given appropriate support.
All children should be encouraged to have a go at spelling each word, using the strategies that they have learnt.
Remind the children to check their answers by asking: *Does it look right? Does it sound right?*
Avoid over-emphasising the spelling of each word as you read it.

> Read each word aloud, saying: *The word is...*
> Next, read the sentence that includes the word.
> Wait for the children to attempt to write the word.
> Re-read the word, saying: *The word is...*

Remind the children to check the word before moving to the next spelling.
At the end of the test, read each sentence again and encourage the children to check back.

Instructions for children

(You may like to read this to the children prior to the test.)

This is a spelling test to check your knowledge of the spelling patterns we have worked on this half term.
You need a pencil.
Please write your name, class and the date at the top of the test.
I will read a word out loud and then say it again in a sentence.
You should write the word in the gap in the sentence on your test.
I will read it again and give you time to check it.
Don't worry if you are not sure about a spelling. Have a go using the strategies we have learnt.
If you make a mistake, cross out the word and try again.

Words tested (10)

bread, her, under, bird, hurt, moon, book, road, mouth, grow

© HarperCollins*Publishers* Ltd 2018

Year 1/P2 Spring Half Term 2 Test A

Spelling script

Spelling 1: The word is **bread**.
Dad slices the **bread** to make toast.
The word is **bread**.

Spelling 2: The word is **her**.
Her eyes were blue.
The word is **her**.

Spelling 3: The word is **under**.
Let's hide **under** the bed.
The word is **under**.

Spelling 4: The word is **bird**.
The **bird** made a nest in the tree.
The word is **bird**.

Spelling 5: The word is **hurt**.
Ouch! I have **hurt** my finger.
The word is **hurt**.

Spelling 6: The word is **moon**.
The **moon** is glowing in the night sky.
The word is **moon**.

Spelling 7: The word is **book**.
The **book** told tales of mystery and adventure.
The word is **book**.

Spelling 8: The word is **road**.
The **road** outside my house is very busy in the morning.
The word is **road**.

Spelling 9: The word is **mouth**.
I have two eyes, one nose and one **mouth**!
The word is **mouth**.

Spelling 10: The word is **grow**.
We eat healthy food to help us **grow**.
The word is **grow**.

Well done! Now I will read the sentences again so you can check your spelling.

| Name | Class | Date |

Year 1/P2 Spring Half Term 2 Test A

1. Dad slices the _____ to make toast.

2. _____ eyes were blue.

3. Let's hide _____ the bed.

4. The _____ made a nest in the tree.

5. Ouch! I have _____ my finger.

6. The _____ is glowing in the night sky.

7. The _____ told tales of mystery and adventure.

8. The _____ outside my house is very busy in the morning.

9. I have two eyes, one nose and one _____!

10. We eat healthy food to help us _____.

Total _____ / 10

Year 1/P2 Spring Half Term 2 Test B

Spelling rules and knowledge

- Vowel digraphs and trigraphs: **ea** (*tread*), **er**, **er** (unstressed schwa), **ir**, **ur**, **oo** (*soon*), **oo** (*good*), **oa**, **ow** (*town*), **ue**

Guidance for teachers

The test is designed to build experience and confidence with this format, as well as to test children's spelling knowledge.
The test should take approximately 10–15 minutes.
Children should have a copy of the test and a pencil to use.
Children with specific needs should be given appropriate support.
All children should be encouraged to have a go at spelling each word, using the strategies that they have learnt.
Remind the children to check their answers by asking: *Does it look right? Does it sound right?*
Avoid over-emphasising the spelling of each word as you read it.

> Read each word aloud, saying: *The word is…*
> Next, read the sentence that includes the word.
> Wait for the children to attempt to write the word.
> Re-read the word, saying: *The word is…*

Remind the children to check the word before moving to the next spelling.
At the end of the test, read each sentence again and encourage the children to check back.

Instructions for children

(You may like to read this to the children prior to the test.)

This is a spelling test to check your knowledge of the spelling patterns we have worked on this half term.
You need a pencil.
Please write your name, class and the date at the top of the test.
I will read a word out loud and then say it again in a sentence.
You should write the word in the gap in the sentence on your test.
I will read it again and give you time to check it.
Don't worry if you are not sure about a spelling. Have a go using the strategies we have learnt.
If you make a mistake, cross out the word and try again.

Words tested (10)

tread, person, sister, third, burst, soon, good, coach, town, blue

Year 1/P2 Spring Half Term 2 Test B

Spelling script

Spelling 1: The word is **tread**.
Try not to **tread** in the mud in your new shoes.
The word is **tread**.

Spelling 2: The word is **person**.
The angry **person** is shouting.
The word is **person.**

Spelling 3: The word is **sister**.
My **sister** is much taller than me.
The word is **sister**.

Spelling 4: The word is **third**.
The **third** runner to finish the race gets a bronze medal.
The word is **third**.

Spelling 5: The word is **burst**.
My balloon **burst** on a prickly leaf!
The word is **burst**.

Spelling 6: The word is **soon**.
Soon it will be tea time.
The word is **soon**.

Spelling 7: The word is **good**.
The **good** puppy didn't pull on its lead.
The word is **good**.

Spelling 8: The word is **coach**.
The children travelled to school on a **coach**.
The word is **coach**.

Spelling 9: The word is **town**.
Our **town** has lots of shops and cafés.
The word is **town**.

Spelling 10: The word is **blue**.
The **blue** whale is the largest sea animal.
The word is **blue**.

Well done! Now I will read the sentences again so you can check your spelling.

| Name | Class | Date |

Year 1/P2 Spring Half Term 2 Test B

1. Try not to _____ in the mud in your new shoes.

2. The angry _____ is shouting.

3. My _____ is much taller than me.

4. The _____ runner to finish the race gets a bronze medal.

5. My balloon _____ on a prickly leaf!

6. _____ it will be tea time.

7. The _____ puppy didn't pull on its lead.

8. The children travelled to school on a _____.

9. Our _____ has lots of shops and cafés.

10. The _____ whale is the largest sea animal.

Total _____ / 10

Year 1/P2 Summer Half Term 1 Test A

Spelling rules and knowledge

- Vowel digraphs and trigraphs: **ew**, **ie** (*pie*), **ie** (*thief*), **igh**, **or**, **aw** (*saw*), **au**, **air**, **ear** (*beard*)

Guidance for teachers

The test is designed to build experience and confidence with this format, as well as to test children's spelling knowledge.
The test should take approximately 10–15 minutes.
Children should have a copy of the test and a pencil to use.
Children with specific needs should be given appropriate support.
All children should be encouraged to have a go at spelling each word, using the strategies that they have learnt.
Remind the children to check their answers by asking: *Does it look right? Does it sound right?*
Avoid over-emphasising the spelling of each word as you read it.

> Read each word aloud, saying: *The word is…*
> Next, read the sentence that includes the word.
> Wait for the children to attempt to write the word.
> Re-read the word, saying: *The word is…*

Remind the children to check the word before moving to the next spelling.
At the end of the test, read each sentence again and encourage the children to check back.

Instructions for children

(You may like to read this to the children prior to the test.)

This is a spelling test to check your knowledge of the spelling patterns we have worked on this half term.
You need a pencil.
Please write your name, class and the date at the top of the test.
I will read a word out loud and then say it again in a sentence.
You should write the word in the gap in the sentence on your test.
I will read it again and give you time to check it.
Don't worry if you are not sure about a spelling. Have a go using the strategies we have learnt.
If you make a mistake, cross out the word and try again.

Words tested (10)

grew, pie, tried, thief, high, short, saw, dinosaur, hair, beard

Year 1/P2 Summer Half Term 1 Test A

Spelling script

Spelling 1: The word is **grew**.
The cactus plant **grew** terrible spikes.
The word is **grew**.

Spelling 2: The word is **pie**.
Apple **pie** tastes yummy with ice cream.
The word is **pie**.

Spelling 3: The word is **tried**.
The girl **tried** to remember her address.
The word is **tried**.

Spelling 4: The word is **thief**.
The naughty **thief** stole sweets from the jar.
The word is **thief**.

Spelling 5: The word is **high**.
How **high** can you jump?
The word is **high**.

Spelling 6: The word is **short**.
My new trousers are too **short**!
The word is **short**.

Spelling 7: The word is **saw**.
We **saw** nurse sharks at the aquarium.
The word is **saw**.

Spelling 8: The word is **dinosaur**.
The friendly **dinosaur** only ate leaves and plants.
The word is **dinosaur**.

Spelling 9: The word is **hair**.
I hate having my **hair** cut!
The word is **hair**.

Spelling 10: The word is **beard**.
My dad grew a bushy **beard**.
The word is **beard**.

Well done! Now I will read the sentences again so you can check your spelling.

| Name | Class | Date |

Year 1/P2 Summer Half Term 1 Test A

1. The cactus plant _____ terrible spikes.

2. Apple _____ tastes yummy with ice cream.

3. The girl _____ to remember her address.

4. The naughty _____ stole sweets from the jar.

5. How _____ can you jump?

6. My new trousers are too _____!

7. We _____ nurse sharks at the aquarium.

8. The friendly _____ only ate leaves and plants.

9. I hate having my _____ cut!

10. My dad grew a bushy _____.

Total _____ / 10

Year 1/P2 Summer Half Term 1 Test B

Spelling rules and knowledge

- Vowel digraphs and trigraphs: **ew**, **ie** (*cried*), **ie** (*shield*), **igh**, **or**, **aw** (*yawn*), **au**, **air**, **ear** (*year*)

Guidance for teachers

The test is designed to build experience and confidence with this format, as well as to test children's spelling knowledge.
The test should take approximately 10–15 minutes.
Children should have a copy of the test and a pencil to use.
Children with specific needs should be given appropriate support.
All children should be encouraged to have a go at spelling each word, using the strategies that they have learnt.
Remind the children to check their answers by asking: *Does it look right? Does it sound right?*
Avoid over-emphasising the spelling of each word as you read it.

> Read each word aloud, saying: *The word is…*
> Next, read the sentence that includes the word.
> Wait for the children to attempt to write the word.
> Re-read the word, saying: *The word is…*

Remind the children to check the word before moving to the next spelling.
At the end of the test, read each sentence again and encourage the children to check back.

Instructions for children

(You may like to read this to the children prior to the test.)

This is a spelling test to check your knowledge of the spelling patterns we have worked on this half term.
You need a pencil.
Please write your name, class and the date at the top of the test.
I will read a word out loud and then say it again in a sentence.
You should write the word in the gap in the sentence on your test.
I will read it again and give you time to check it.
Don't worry if you are not sure about a spelling. Have a go using the strategies we have learnt.
If you make a mistake, cross out the word and try again.

Words tested (10)

crew, cried, shield, fright, horse, shore, yawn, astronaut, chair, year

Year 1/P2 Summer Half Term 1 Test B

Spelling script

Spelling 1: The word is **crew**.
The pirate **crew** shouted, "Land ahoy!"
The word is **crew**.

Spelling 2: The word is **cried**.
The baby **cried** when he lost his teddy.
The word is **cried**.

Spelling 3: The word is **shield**.
The knight protected himself with his **shield** and sword.
The word is **shield**.

Spelling 4: The word is **fright**.
Ooh! You gave me a **fright**!
The word is **fright**.

Spelling 5: The word is **horse**.
The **horse** galloped to its stable.
The word is **horse**.

Spelling 6: The word is **shore**.
The crabs walked sideways to the sea **shore**.
The word is **shore**.

Spelling 7: The word is **yawn**.
When I am tired, I **yawn** my head off!
The word is **yawn**.

Spelling 8: The word is **astronaut**.
The **astronaut** climbed into the spaceship.
The word is **astronaut**.

Spelling 9: The word is **chair**.
I broke the leg of my **chair**!
The word is **chair**.

Spelling 10: The word is **year**.
Next **year**, I will begin guitar lessons.
The word is **year**.

Well done! Now I will read the sentences again so you can check your spelling.

| Name | Class | Date |

Year 1/P2 Summer Half Term 1 Test B

1. The pirate _____ shouted, "Land ahoy!"

2. The baby _____ when he lost his teddy.

3. The knight protected himself with his _____ and sword.

4. Ooh! You gave me a _____!

5. The _____ galloped to its stable.

6. The crabs walked sideways to the sea _____.

7. When I am tired, I _____ my head off!

8. The _____ climbed into the spaceship.

9. I broke the leg of my _____!

10. Next _____, I will begin guitar lessons.

Total _____ / 10

Year 1/P2 Summer Half Term 2 Test A

Spelling rules and knowledge

- Vowel digraphs and trigraphs: **ear** (*bear*), **are** (*care*)
- Words ending **-y**
- New consonant spellings **ph** and **wh**
- The sound made by **k**
- Compound words
- Common exception words

Guidance for teachers

The test is designed to build experience and confidence with this format, as well as to test children's spelling knowledge.
The test should take approximately 10–15 minutes.
Children should have a copy of the test and a pencil to use.
Children with specific needs should be given appropriate support.
All children should be encouraged to have a go at spelling each word, using the strategies that they have learnt.
Remind the children to check their answers by asking: *Does it look right? Does it sound right?*
Avoid over-emphasising the spelling of each word as you read it.

> Read each word aloud, saying: *The word is…*
> Next, read the sentence that includes the word.
> Wait for the children to attempt to write the word.
> Re-read the word, saying: *The word is…*

Remind the children to check the word before moving to the next spelling.
At the end of the test, read each sentence again and encourage the children to check back.

Instructions for children

(You may like to read this to the children prior to the test.)

This is a spelling test to check your knowledge of the spelling patterns we have worked on this half term.
You need a pencil.
Please write your name, class and the date at the top of the test.
I will read a word out loud and then say it again in a sentence.
You should write the word in the gap in the sentence on your test.
I will read it again and give you time to check it.
Don't worry if you are not sure about a spelling. Have a go using the strategies we have learnt.
If you make a mistake, cross out the word and try again.

Words tested (10)

bear, care, happy, dolphin, when, skin, playground, what, one, school

Year 1/P2 Summer Half Term 2 Test A

Spelling script

Spelling 1: The word is **bear**.
The hungry **bear** hunted for fish.
The word is **bear**.

Spelling 2: The word is **care**.
We **care** for our pets.
The word is **care**.

Spelling 3: The word is **happy**.
The **happy** monkey ate its banana.
The word is **happy**.

Spelling 4: The word is **dolphin**.
The **dolphin** swam through the waves.
The word is **dolphin**.

Spelling 5: The word is **when**.
When is your birthday?
The word is **when**.

Spelling 6: The word is **skin**.
Snakes shed their **skin** when they grow.
The word is **skin**.

Spelling 7: The word is **playground**.
The **playground** has a shiny new slide.
The word is **playground**.

Spelling 8: The word is **what**.
What is the time, please?
The word is **what**.

Spelling 9: The word is **one**.
One, two, three, four, five!
The word is **one**.

Spelling 10: The word is **school**.
The **school** teacher smiled at the children.
The word is **school**.

Well done! Now I will read the sentences again so you can check your spelling.

| Name | Class | Date |

Year 1/P2 Summer Half Term 2 Test A

1. The hungry _____ hunted for fish.

2. We _____ for our pets.

3. The _____ monkey ate its banana.

4. The _____ swam through the waves.

5. _____ is your birthday?

6. Snakes shed their _____ when they grow.

7. The _____ has a shiny new slide.

8. _____ is the time, please?

9. _____, two, three, four, five!

10. The _____ teacher smiled at the children.

Total _____ / 10

Year 1/P2 Summer Half Term 2 Test B

Spelling rules and knowledge

- Vowel digraphs and trigraphs: **ear** (*wear*), **are** (*care*)
- Words ending **-y**
- New consonant spellings **ph** and **wh**
- The sound made by **k**
- Compound words
- Common exception words

Guidance for teachers

The test is designed to build experience and confidence with this format, as well as to test children's spelling knowledge.
The test should take approximately 10–15 minutes.
Children should have a copy of the test and a pencil to use.
Children with specific needs should be given appropriate support.
All children should be encouraged to have a go at spelling each word, using the strategies that they have learnt.
Remind the children to check their answers by asking: *Does it look right? Does it sound right?*
Avoid over-emphasising the spelling of each word as you read it.

> Read each word aloud, saying: *The word is…*
> Next, read the sentence that includes the word.
> Wait for the children to attempt to write the word.
> Re-read the word, saying: *The word is…*

Remind the children to check the word before moving to the next spelling.
At the end of the test, read each sentence again and encourage the children to check back.

Instructions for children

(You may like to read this to the children prior to the test.)

This is a spelling test to check your knowledge of the spelling patterns we have worked on this half term.
You need a pencil.
Please write your name, class and the date at the top of the test.
I will read a word out loud and then say it again in a sentence.
You should write the word in the gap in the sentence on your test.
I will read it again and give you time to check it.
Don't worry if you are not sure about a spelling. Have a go using the strategies we have learnt.
If you make a mistake, cross out the word and try again.

Words tested (10)

wear, glare, family, elephant, where, kit, bedroom, why, friend, once

Year 1/P2 Summer Half Term 2 Test B

Spelling script

Spelling 1: The word is **wear**.
The prince loved to **wear** his crown.
The word is **wear**.

Spelling 2: The word is **glare**.
The **glare** of the creature's eyes was terrible.
The word is **glare**.

Spelling 3: The word is **family**.
The **family** enjoy going to the zoo together.
The word is **family**.

Spelling 4: The word is **elephant**.
The **elephant** sprayed the crowd with its trunk.
The word is **elephant**.

Spelling 5: The word is **where**.
Where are you hiding?
The word is **where**.

Spelling 6: The word is **kit**.
We pack our sports **kit** in our PE bag.
The word is **kit**.

Spelling 7: The word is **bedroom**.
I keep my toys in my **bedroom**.
The word is **bedroom**.

Spelling 8: The word is **why**.
Why is the sky blue?
The word is **why**.

Spelling 9: The word is **friend**.
Would your **friend** like to play with us?
The word is **friend**.

Spelling 10: The word is **once**.
Once upon a time…
The word is **once**.

Well done! Now I will read the sentences again so you can check your spelling.

| Name | Class | Date |

Year 1/P2 Summer Half Term 2 Test B

1. The prince loved to _____ his crown.

2. The _____ of the creature's eyes was terrible.

3. The _____ enjoy going to the zoo together.

4. The _____ sprayed the crowd with its trunk.

5. _____ are you hiding?

6. We pack our sports _____ in our PE bag.

7. I keep my toys in my _____.

8. _____ is the sky blue?

9. Would your _____ like to play with us?

10. _____ upon a time…

Total _____ / 10

Answers in Context

Year 1/P2 Autumn Half Term 1 Test A

1. Eat **the** cake.

2. The teacher **said**, "Hurry up!"

3. Can **you** play the drums?

4. Come **here** and sit down.

5. The cat can jump **off** the bed.

Answers in Context

Year 1/P2 Autumn Half Term 1 Test B

1. **Do** you like chocolate?

2. He **was** feeling scared.

3. **They** are best friends.

4. We **love** our kitten.

5. The wasp gave an angry **buzz**.

Answers in Context

Year 1/P2 Autumn Half Term 2 Test A

1. Be careful! The river **bank** may be slippery.

2. Can we **catch** the fish?

3. **Have** you eaten your vegetables?

4. She **spends** her time playing on the computer.

5. The tiger **hunted** for its prey.

6. The **slowest** runner came last in the race.

Answers in Context

Year 1/P2 Autumn Half Term 2 Test B

1. The elephant's **trunk** snatched the doughnut.

2. The dog loved to **fetch** its ball.

3. One, two, three, four, **five**!

4. The **rocks** at the beach were hard to climb.

5. The kangaroo was **jumping** along the road.

6. My kitten's fur is **softer** than my teddy bear.

Answers in Context

Year 1/P2 Spring Half Term 1 Test A

1. The **rain** washed the mud off the wellies.

2. The shiny **coin** gleamed in my purse.

3. Let's **play** hide and seek.

4. The **boy** loved his new trainers.

5. The cheeky robin **came** close to my window.

6. Whose smelly socks are **these**?

7. The camel **ride** was very bumpy!

8. She **woke** up with a jump when the doorbell rang.

9. The king liked to **rule** over his kingdom.

10. The squirrels climbed up their favourite **tree** every morning.

Answers in Context

Year 1/P2 Spring Half Term 1 Test B

1. The **train** chugged into the tunnel.

2. We dug in the **soil** to plant our seeds.

3. The boys ran **away** from the barking dog.

4. I **enjoy** a cream cake with a cup of tea.

5. My new shoes are the **same** as yours.

6. Ouch! I stubbed my **toe** on the doorstep.

7. Put your shoes on at the **side** of the football pitch.

8. We **hope** that we can play outside today.

9. Toot your horn when you **start** the car.

10. I like to **dream** that I am on a beautiful beach.

Answers in Context

Year 1/P2 Spring Half Term 2 Test A

1. Dad slices the **bread** to make toast.

2. **Her** eyes were blue.

3. Let's hide **under** the bed.

4. The **bird** made a nest in the tree.

5. Ouch! I have **hurt** my finger.

6. The **moon** is glowing in the night sky.

7. The **book** told tales of mystery and adventure.

8. The **road** outside my house is very busy in the morning.

9. I have two eyes, one nose and one **mouth**!

10. We eat healthy food to help us **grow**.

Answers in Context

Year 1/P2 Spring Half Term 2 Test B

1. Try not to **tread** in the mud in your new shoes.

2. The angry **person** is shouting.

3. My **sister** is much taller than me.

4. The **third** runner to finish the race gets a bronze medal.

5. My balloon **burst** on a prickly leaf!

6. **Soon** it will be tea time.

7. The **good** puppy didn't pull on its lead.

8. The children travelled to school on a **coach**.

9. Our **town** has lots of shops and cafés.

10. The **blue** whale is the largest sea animal.

Answers in Context

Year 1/P2 Summer Half Term 1 Test A

1. The cactus plant **grew** terrible spikes.

2. Apple **pie** tastes yummy with ice cream.

3. The girl **tried** to remember her address.

4. The naughty **thief** stole sweets from the jar.

5. How **high** can you jump?

6. My new trousers are too **short**!

7. We **saw** nurse sharks at the aquarium.

8. The friendly **dinosaur** only ate leaves and plants.

9. I hate having my **hair** cut!

10. My dad grew a bushy **beard**.

Answers in Context

Year 1/P2 Summer Half Term 1 Test B

1. The pirate **crew** shouted, "Land ahoy!"

2. The baby **cried** when he lost his teddy.

3. The knight protected himself with his **shield** and sword.

4. Ooh! You gave me a **fright**!

5. The **horse** galloped to its stable.

6. The crabs walked sideways to the sea **shore**.

7. When I am tired, I **yawn** my head off!

8. The **astronaut** climbed into the spaceship.

9. I broke the leg of my **chair**!

10. Next **year**, I will begin guitar lessons.

Answers in Context

Year 1/P2 Summer Half Term 2 Test A

1. The hungry **bear** hunted for fish.

2. We **care** for our pets.

3. The **happy** monkey ate its banana.

4. The **dolphin** swam through the waves.

5. **When** is your birthday?

6. Snakes shed their **skin** when they grow.

7. The **playground** has a shiny new slide.

8. **What** is the time, please?

9. **One**, two, three, four, five!

10. The **school** teacher smiled at the children.

Answers in Context

Year 1/P2 Summer Half Term 2 Test B

1. The prince loved to **wear** his crown.

2. The **glare** of the creature's eyes was terrible.

3. The **family** enjoy going to the zoo together.

4. The **elephant** sprayed the crowd with its trunk.

5. **Where** are you hiding?

6. We pack our sports **kit** in our PE bag.

7. I keep my toys in my **bedroom**.

8. **Why** is the sky blue?

9. Would your **friend** like to play with us?

10. **Once** upon a time...

Word-only Answers

Year 1/P2 Autumn Half Term 1 Test A
1. the, 2. said, 3. you, 4. here, 5. off

Year 1/P2 Autumn Half Term 1 Test B
1. do, 2. was, 3. they, 4. love, 5. buzz

Year 1/P2 Autumn Half Term 2 Test A
1. bank, 2. catch, 3. have, 4. spends, 5. hunted, 6. slowest

Year 1/P2 Autumn Half Term 2 Test B
1. trunk, 2. fetch, 3. five, 4. rocks, 5. jumping, 6. softer

Year 1/P2 Spring Half Term 1 Test A
1. rain, 2. coin, 3. play, 4. boy, 5. came, 6. these, 7. ride, 8. woke, 9. rule, 10. tree

Year 1/P2 Spring Half Term 1 Test B
1. train, 2. soil, 3. away, 4. enjoy, 5. same, 6. toe, 7. side, 8. hope, 9. start, 10. dream

Year 1/P2 Spring Half Term 2 Test A
1. bread, 2. her, 3. under, 4. bird, 5. hurt, 6. moon, 7. book, 8. road, 9. mouth, 10. grow

Year 1/P2 Spring Half Term 2 Test B
1. tread, 2. person, 3. sister, 4. third, 5. burst, 6. soon, 7. good, 8. coach, 9. town, 10. blue

Year 1/P2 Summer Half Term 1 Test A
1. grew, 2. pie, 3. tried, 4. thief, 5. high, 6. short, 7. saw, 8. dinosaur, 9. hair, 10. beard

Year 1/P2 Summer Half Term 1 Test B
1. crew, 2. cried, 3. shield, 4. fright, 5. horse, 6. shore, 7. yawn, 8. astronaut, 9. chair, 10. year

Year 1/P2 Summer Half Term 2 Test A
1. bear, 2. care, 3. happy, 4. dolphin, 5. when, 6. skin, 7. playground, 8. what, 9. one, 10. school

Year 1/P2 Summer Half Term 2 Test B
1. wear, 2. glare, 3. family, 4. elephant, 5. where, 6. kit, 7. bedroom, 8. why, 9. friend, 10. once

© HarperCollins*Publishers* Ltd 2018

Name	Class

Year 1/P2 Spelling Record Sheet

Tests	Mark	Total marks	Key words to target
Autumn Half Term 1 Test A		5	
Autumn Half Term 1 Test B		5	
Autumn Half Term 2 Test A		6	
Autumn Half Term 2 Test B		6	
Spring Half Term 1 Test A		10	
Spring Half Term 1 Test B		10	
Spring Half Term 2 Test A		10	
Spring Half Term 2 Test B		10	
Summer Half Term 1 Test A		10	
Summer Half Term 1 Test B		10	
Summer Half Term 2 Test A		10	
Summer Half Term 2 Test B		10	

© HarperCollins*Publishers* Ltd 2018